love yo

VICTORIA
JUSTICE

Jenny Vaughan

LONDON·SYDNEY

First published in 2012 by
Franklin Watts
338 Euston Road
London NW1 3BH

Franklin Watts Australia
Level 17/207 Kent Street
Sydney NSW 2000

Series editor: Adrian Cole
Art direction: Peter Scoulding
Design: Simon Borrough
Picture research: Diana Morris

Acknowledgements:

Broadimage/Rex Features: 17. Chris Delmas/Starstock/Photoshot: 10. Helga
Estab/Shutterstock: front cover, 21t, 22. Charles Gallay/WireImage/Getty
Images: 12, 14, 27. Jesse Grant/WireImage/Getty Images: 4. Roadell Hickman/
Zuma Press/Corbis: 19. Justin Hyte/Corbis: 28-29. Henry Lamb/Photowire/Rex
Features: 24. Music4mix/Shutterstock: 26. © Nic/Everett/Rex Features: 5, 15. ©
Nickelodeon: 9, 11, 13. Gregory Pace/BEI/Rex Features: 20. Christopher Polk/
Getty Images: 18, 23. Roy Sonobel/Retna/Corbis: 16. Startracks/Rex Features:
7. Kevin Winter/Getty Images: 25. © Zooey Magazine: 21b.

Every attempt has been made to clear copyright. Should there be any inadvertent
omission please apply to the publisher for rectification.

A CIP catalogue record for this book
is available from the British Library.

ISBN: 978 1 4451 0658 8

Printed in China

Franklin Watts is a division of Hachette
Children's Books, an Hachette UK company.
www.hachette.co.uk

Contents

Words highlighted in the text can be found in the glossary.

Meet
Victoria

Victoria Justice is incredibly talented. She's an actress, model, singer and songwriter. She's best known for her Nickelodeon show *Victorious*. Before that she played Lola Martinez in *Zoey 101*, which ran from 2005 to 2008.

Victoria appears at an awards ceremony in 2005.

Victorious was first shown in the US in March 2010. It's a comedy about "Tori" (Victoria) Vegas, who attends a school for the performing arts.

Victorious gets between about 4 and 6 million viewers each time it's shown. It's made Victoria one of US TV's richest young stars – in 2010 she was paid around $12,000 for each episode.

The **pilot episode** of *Victorious.*

For Victoria, music is part of her life. Her TV work has meant she has to sing and dance. She also writes songs, and is just setting out on a solo career.

Who is Victoria?

Victoria Dawn Justice was born on 19 February, 1993 – her star sign is Pisces. She was born in Hollywood. That's not the famous Hollywood in California, but a town in Florida with the same name.

Victoria's mother, Serene, is from Puerto Rico. Zack, her father, is part Irish. Her parents are now divorced and she lives in Los Angeles with her mother and her stepfather, Mark Reed.

Victoria was only eight years old when she decided she wanted to be on television. Her mother sent some photos to modelling agencies, and she was signed up.

She was soon starring in commercials. By the time she was 11, she'd been in over 30 of them. She's modelled for top clothes labels, including Ralph Lauren and Gap.

Victoria and her mother Serene Justice in 2010.

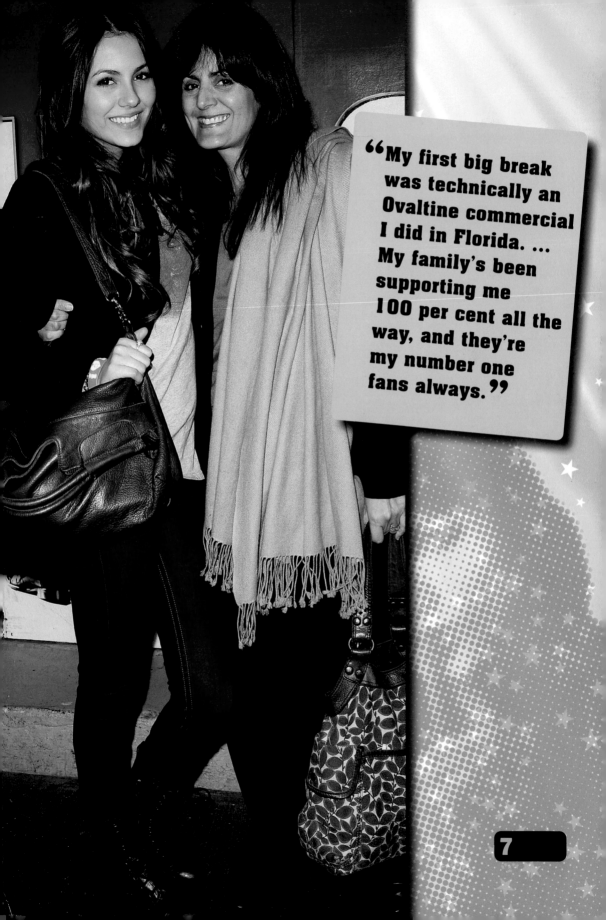

66My first big break was technically an Ovaltine commercial I did in Florida. ... My family's been supporting me 100 per cent all the way, and they're my number one fans always.99

To Hollywood

In 2003, Victoria's parents took her to Hollywood, Los Angeles, for the summer. She played the part of a hobbit in an episode of a show called *The Gilmore Girls*.

The next year, the family moved to Los Angeles full-time. Her mother says, "We came for the summer – and we never went back!"

"I wasn't always confident. That's something I've grown into and am still working on. I still have so many insecurities that I'm trying to grow out of."

Victoria got a place at a school there that specialised in the performing arts. Students also studied ordinary subjects. Victoria did well – but she admits she really didn't like maths! And juggling school with work was hard.

In 2005, she was guest star in the Disney show *The Suite Life of Zack and Cody*. Then, in the same year, she got her big breakthrough – a starring part in Nickelodeon's *Zoey 101*.

The cover of a soundtrack CD featuring the cast of *Zoey 101*. Victoria is fourth from the left.

Zoey 101

Victoria was 12 years old when she auditioned for the part of Lola Martinez in *Zoey 101*. She was a co-star until it ended in 2008.

Victoria and Jamie Lynn Spears share a joke at a movie **premiere** in 2006.

Victoria said being in *Zoey 101* was fun. She had two favourite episodes. In one, she had to dress as a boy: "That was an interesting experience ... getting into character, studying my guy friends." And the other? "I got to mud-wrestle Jamie Lynn Spears!"

She also began to build up a fan base. Once, a girl turned up dressed as Lola, in a ballet skirt and jeans. "She wanted me to autograph the skirt!"

Zoey 101 was produced by Dan Schneider. He's made many successful "tween" (young teen) shows for Nickelodeon. After he had seen Victoria in *Zoey*, he told his bosses, "I've got your next star."

The *Zoey 101* cast – in 2007 – looking all grown up!

Victoria in the movies

Victoria's big screen career began in 2005, with two short films, *Mary* (about a girl who sees a vision of the Virgin Mary) and *My Purple Fur Coat*. She was also in a family comedy, *When Do We Eat?*

Victoria in the make-up department.

In 2006, she was in a thriller, *Unknown*, and a horror movie, *The Garden*. In 2009, she had a leading part in *The Kings of Appletown* with Colin and Dylan Sprouse. "It was really fun – they're like normal teenage boys – they're so down-to-earth … so funny."

She has also been in made-for-TV movies: including *Silver Bells* in 2005 and *The Boy Who Cried Werewolf* in 2009. A musical, *Spectacular!* (2009), gave her the chance to sing and dance. She's made guest appearances in other TV series, including three episodes of *iCarly*.

She's also in two other films – *Fun Size*, about a girl whose little brother goes missing, and a comedy romance, *The First Time*.

Victoria, complete with werewolf hand, in a poster for her movie *The Boy Who Cried Werewolf*.

"My dream co-star would have to be Johnny Depp!"

Victorious

Victorious is a comedy set in a performing arts high school. The show was partly Victoria's own idea. It came up at a meeting with producer Dan Schneider.

> **"I said, 'Well, I went to a performing arts middle school ... maybe we can do something with that?' Dan thought it was a great idea ..."**

Victoria and the cast of *Victorious* perform "All I Want Is Everything" before greeting fans in 2011.

Victoria and
some of the cast from the
first **season** of *Victorious*.

The first episode of *Victorious*
was shown in the US in March
2010, and nearly 6 million
people watched. Since then,
Victorious has regularly had
more than three million
viewers for each episode.

Music is important in *Victorious*
– and Victoria has been able to
use her skills as a songwriter.
She co-wrote the show's theme
"Make It Shine" and others,
including her own favourite,
"Best Friend's Brother".

66 ...like my character,
once I got on stage,
I just completely
forgot about
everything – I was
so in the zone
... I loved every
second. 99

15

At home

Victoria lives with her mother, stepfather, Mark, and younger sister, Madison. She's very grateful to her parents for making the move across the US for her – and she hopes to pay them back for everything they have done for her.

Victoria attends a Lakers basketball game in 2011.

Victoria is very close to her mother – who is also her manager. She says she asks her advice on everything – from work to boyfriends.

Victoria out and about in Hollywood, in 2011.

❝But even more important, my mom is kind, compassionate, accepting, and attentive — the type of person you always want to have around.❞

Many of her friends are young stars like herself – but she keeps her feet on the ground.

❝I love hanging out with my friends. We go to the movies a lot. I love eating, so I'm always trying to find new restaurants. I love really good food. ... I ride my bike in my neighbourhood. I make YouTube videos for my friends for fun.❞

17

Singing career

Victorious did more than make Victoria a big star. It also made her realise just how important music was to her. "It's something that's just been in my blood."

The pilot of the show was the moment where she realised, "Woah, this is something that I can actually do for the rest of my life and maybe be successful at."

So far, she has released albums of songs from *Victorious* and *Spectacular!* She's also released five singles from *Victorious* – "Make It Shine", "Freak The Freak Out", "Beggin' On Your Knees", "Best Friend's Brother" and "I Want You Back".

Victoria performs during the 2011 Kids' Choice Awards.

Now she's planning a solo album, which she says will take a new direction. It'll be "more mature", she says. "I'm finding my own path."

Victoria with a young fan at a signing event in Ohio, USA, 2011.

"I like writing songs about things that are real to me and things that I care about, so when other people hear them, they're like, 'I'm going through the exact same thing.'"

Victoria  style

As a model (as well as an actress and singer) Victoria has a great sense of fashion and style. Her favourite style is casual.

One of her "trademarks" is the clever way she uses accessories. She loves bracelets, scarves and boots – and big floppy hats for sunny days.

Victoria tries out earrings at Olive and Bette's in New York.

Of course, she can look amazingly glamorous at awards ceremonies and other big show business occasions. And, as a model, she's in demand for fashion shoots.

Victoria in a stunning silver dress at the 42nd NAACP Image Awards.

Victoria on the cover of Zooey Magazine.

In 2010 she appeared in Zooey Magazine dressed in the style of Audrey Hepburn – a big star in the 1950s and 1960s. She especially loves the style worn by actress Sienna Miller.

Awards
and prizes

Award ceremonies are nothing new for Victoria – and she's already been part of a winning team. Back in 2006 and 2007, she was part of the *Zoey 101* team that won a Young Artist Award.

Victoria poses for cameras before the start of the Kids' Choice Awards 2011.

In 2011 she was nominated for a Young Artist Award for her leading role as Jordan Sands, in *The Boy Who Cried Werewolf*. She's also already had several nominations for awards for *Victorious*.

A high point came in April 2011. She hosted the Kids' Choice Awards – where she also had a nomination for her part in *Victorious*. She wore an amazing mini-dress (shown above).

22

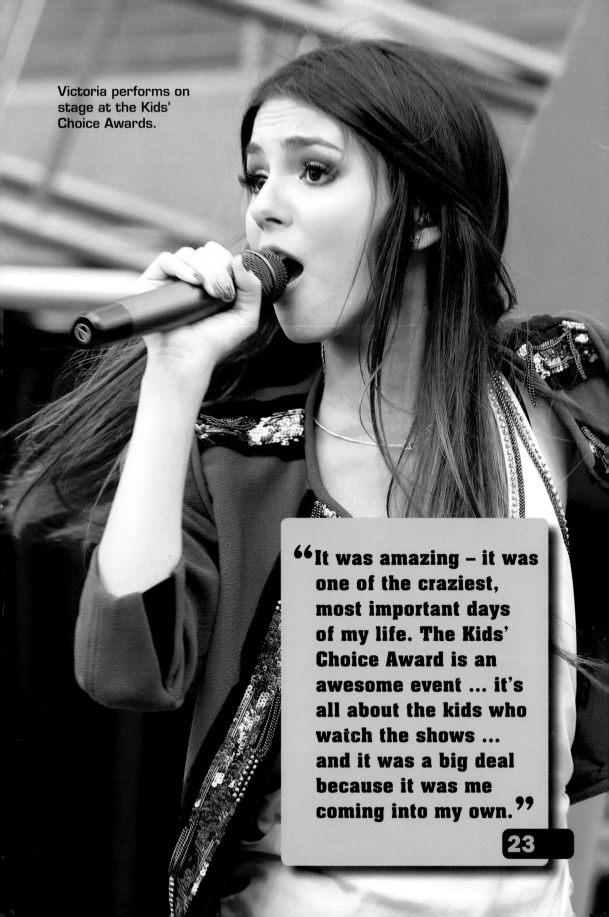

Victoria performs on stage at the Kids' Choice Awards.

"It was amazing – it was one of the craziest, most important days of my life. The Kids' Choice Award is an awesome event ... it's all about the kids who watch the shows ... and it was a big deal because it was me coming into my own."

23

Getting involved

"**Girl Up**" **is a campaign in the US aimed at helping American girls to support girls in** developing countries. **It is part of the UN organisation, The United Nations Foundation.**

Victoria became a Girl Up celebrity champion in 2010. In 2011, she went to Guatemala to see its work there. "It's am amazing cause, and I'm so passionate about it!" she said.

You can read about "Girl Up" at: http://www.girlup.org/about/about-the-un-foundation.html

The "Girl Up" campaign is launched by Victoria in September 2010.

24

In Guatemala, Victoria travelled to some very remote areas and met girls who were learning important lessons about health – as well as how to read and how to speak up for themselves.

She has also been involved with the "Do Something" awards, which honour young people working for social change.

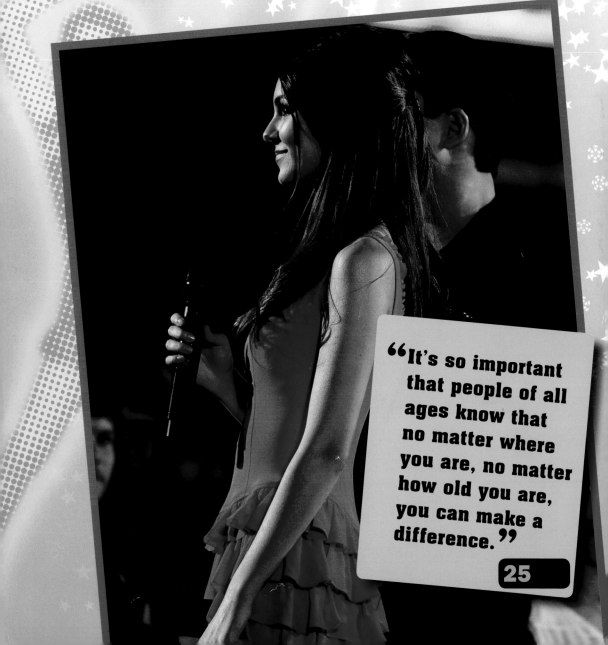

Victoria speaks onstage during the 2011 Do Something awards.

"It's so important that people of all ages know that no matter where you are, no matter how old you are, you can make a difference."

Life in the spotlight

Victoria tells her fans "never let anyone take away your dream". She has certainly been able to live hers and, most of the time, she enjoys being famous. She says it's cool that people want her autograph, and want to take pictures of her.

She says she tries to remember that she's a **role model** for her young fans. Many of them are young teenagers. "I'm not going to do something they wouldn't be able to do," she says.

26

Victoria poses for a fan photo.

Victoria gives a fan
a free hug!

Her advice to young people who
want to follow in her footsteps:
"You have to find ways to keep
training in your local area. There
are always theatre groups, local
acting classes, vocal and dance
classes, which will all help."

But there is a down side to being
famous – and that is not being
able to get away from the **media**.
It is sometimes "quite scary".

"The Internet and
social media
networks have
really exploded
and there's so
much focus
on everyone's
personal life."

Where next?

What does the future hold for Victoria? Her producer, Dan Schneider, says that he thinks that in five years she'll be one of the biggest stars in the world.

Victoria will definitely keep on supporting the Girl Up campaign.

But what will she be doing? She wants to be a movie star and a singer too, she says. "I want it all – why not?"

"I am really passionate about it. I feel like it will work out."

28

Many child stars have a difficult time as they get older. Yet Victoria does seem to be able to keep her feet on the ground. She says that problems can happen to young people in show business "if you get lost in it – when it becomes your world. It's just a job."

It is one that, so far, she's been very successful in. It's hard work but she loves it so much "it doesn't feel like working".

She hopes she'll be able to buy a house for her parents, and continue to make her way in show business.

Fan guide

Full Name: Victoria Dawn Justice
Date of birth: 19 February 1993
Height: 1.7 metres
Hometown: Hollywood, Florida, USA
Record Label: Columbia Records and
Sony Music Entertainment
Colour of eyes: Brown
Hobbies: Reading, ice skating, swimming
and hanging out with her friends

There are many sites about Victoria, and often they let you contribute to discussions about her. Remember, though, that it's OK to make comments, but it's not fair to be unkind. She cannot answer your comments herself!

http://www.victoriajustice.net

http://www.victoriajusticefan.org

http://www.tv.com/people/
victoria-justice/
http://victoriajusticestyle.org/

http://www.teenspot.com/
spotlight/victoria-justice/

http://www.girlup.org/about/
champions-advocates/victoria-
justice.html

http://www.youtube.com/
watch?v=W9PqxaNUTyA

http://www.youtube.com/
watch?v=JZOGt9QxTHk

Please note: every effort has been made by the Publishers to ensure that these websites contain no inappropriate or offensive material. However, because of the nature of the Internet, it is impossible to guarantee that the contents of these sites will not be altered. We strongly advise that Internet access is supervised by a responsible adult.

19 February 1993	Victoria Justice is born
2003	Plays Jill in the TV series *The Gilmore Girls*
2005	Appears as Rebecca in *The Suite Life of Zack and Cody*
	Makes film debut in *Mary*, and also appears in *When Do We Eat?* and *Silver Bells*
2005–2008	Plays Lola Martinez in the TV series *Zoey 101*
2006	Plays Holly in *The Garden*, and also appears in *Unknown*
	Appears as Thalia Thompson in TV series *Everwood*
2009	Plays Tammi Dyson in *Spectacular!* and also appears in *The Kings of Appletown*
	Soundtrack album to *Spectacular!* series is released featuring songs by the cast, which included Victoria Justice
	Appears as Shelby Marx in TV series *iCarly*
2010	Stars as Jordan Sands in *The Boy Who Cried Werewolf*
	Appears as Eris Fairy in TV series *The Troop*
	Nominated for Iconic TV Actress at J-14's Teen Icon Awards
	Releases songs "Make It Shine" and "Freak The Freak Out"
2010– 2011	Plays Tori Vega in the TV series *Victorious*
	Nominated for Favourite TV Actress at Kids' Choice Awards
	Appears as Tori Vega in TV series *iCarly*
	Soundtrack album to *Victorious* series is released featuring songs performed by Tori Vega (the character played by Victoria Justice)
	Releases the songs "Beggin' On Your Knees", "Best Friend's Brother", "I Want You Back" and "All I Want Is Everything"
2012	Stars as Wren in *Fun Size*

Glossary

Developing countries Countries that are poorer than, for example, the US and Europe, and where many people live on very low wages.

Media Used in this way to mean newspaper and TV reporters, as well as photographers.

Performing arts Acting, singing, dancing and performing music.

Pilot episode The first episode of a TV show which is used to see how successful further episodes might be.

Premiere First cinema or TV showing.

Producer The person who is responsible for the overall running of a show.

Role model Someone whom others look up to and want to be like.

Season A set of episodes of a particular TV series.

Virgin Mary The mother of Jesus Christ.

Index